NORTH AMERICAN WILDLIFE

MOOSE

by Jenny Mason

Kaleidoscope
Minneapolis, MN

The Quest for Discovery Never Ends

This edition first published in 2024 by Kaleidoscope Publishing, Inc.

For information regarding permission, write to
Kaleidoscope Publishing, Inc.
6012 Blue Circle Drive
Minnetonka, MN 55343

Library of Congress Control Number
2023936910

ISBN
978-1-64519-727-0 (library bound)
978-1-64519-775-1 (ebook)

Printed in the United States of America.

Bigfoot lurks within one of the images in this book. It's up to you to find him!

TABLE OF CONTENTS

Chapter 1

BIG, BIG, BIG

Snap! Crack! A bull moose crushes forest shrubs. Three features stand out on every moose. First, their huge antlers. They look like paddles with spikes. Some antlers measure almost seven feet (2.1 m) tip-to-tip!

The moose's body is also huge. It holds in heat during icy winters. Long legs protect moose from **predators**. They trot over rocks and snow. Last but not least is the big moose nose, or muzzle. The muzzle is like a thumb. Muscle fibers inside grip and gather food.

Antlers are made of bone. Horns are made of keratin, which is also in hair and nails.

Moose are members of the deer family. They are related to elk and mule deer. They are the largest deer in the world. Most moose measure six to seven feet (1.8–2.1 m) tall at the shoulder. They weigh up to 1,800 pounds (816 kg). That is almost as much as a box truck. Their coat colors are dark brown. Some are reddish gold. Bulls have black muzzles. Females, or cows, have cocoa-colored snouts.

FUN FACT

Moose have two toes. This makes them cousins to giraffes.

In the forest, the bull moose drops his **scat**. The pellets look like almonds covered in chocolate. His large ears perk up suddenly. Moose have excellent hearing and sense of smell. Their eyes see in all directions at all times. The bull scans the forest, making sure he is alone. Moose avoid other moose. They are very shy animals.

BELLS, ROPES, AND SADDLES

Bulls grow dewlaps, or "bells." These are floppy bags under their necks. Stringy "ropes" sometimes hang from bells. Bells and ropes spread a bull's scent. The bright patch of hair on a moose's back is called a saddle. Lots of time in the Sun brightens a moose's coat.

Chapter 2

HOME ON THE TAIGA

A moose calf follows its mother. They cross a muddy taiga, or swamp. It is spring. Biting bugs buzz. Moose live in northern regions in North America. Snowmelt creates boggy wetlands. The cow and calf crunch on the willow stalks that grow here. There are four types of moose. Alaskan moose are the largest. Shiras moose are the smallest. Eastern and Northwestern moose have slimmer antler paddles.

FUN FACT

Moose arrived in North America 10,000 years ago. They moved from Siberia to Alaska.

EAT, REP-EAT

Moose have four stomach chambers. Each one digests tough plant fibers. Moose eat fast. They find a safe place to lie down later. Then they burp up their meal. They slowly chew it into pulp. They swallow the green mush. Other chambers digest the mush.

The cow and calf climb a mountain slope. In winter, an **avalanche** cleared away the trees. Wildflowers grew in their place. Avalanche slopes, floodplains, burn scars, and logging areas are great **habitats** for moose. Can you guess why? They are regularly damaged. Fresh and juicy plants grow in these areas. Moose eat them to survive.

Where Do MOOSE Live?

The moose calf sees a lake. It charges into the water. Moose love water. It cools them. They escape from bugs too. Moose swim in lakes and ponds and the ocean. Moose can squeeze their noses shut underwater. Moose can dive 18 feet (5.5 m) deep. They like to eat soggy lake weeds. These plants are full of salts and minerals. After a swim, the cow and calf must move on. This is the season when their lives change completely.

Moose can swim faster than a person paddling a canoe.

Chapter 3

ONE MOOSE YEAR

The cow chases her calf away. She nips and kicks. This is no game. The calf is a **yearling**. That means it is almost one year old. It must now fend for itself. By late May and early June, cows birth new calves. They need protection from predators. About half of all calves die before they are two months old. Season and survival shape every moose's life.

DANGERS LURKING

Predators hunt old or sick moose. Healthy adult moose are too big. Wolves, bears, and mountain lions attack young moose. Cows defend calves by kicking. One kick can kill a wolf. Ticks are a bigger threat. More than 120,000 ticks can cover a moose. They suck its blood. They pass on diseases.

FUN FACT

Moose calves are North America's fastest growing land animals. In four to five months, they grow from about 30 to 300 pounds (13–136 kg).

After calving season, moose **migrate** to a summer range. Moose feast all summer. They can gobble 40 pounds (18 kg) of plants each day. They need fat to survive the winter. Cows make 55 gallons (208 L) of milk for calves.

Bulls must grow new antlers. They fall off, or shed, in winter. Moose antlers are the fastest growing tissues in the animal kingdom. They gain eight inches (20 cm) each week.

In the fall, many bulls gather in a frosty meadow. They circle each other. They wag their paddles. They groan and grunt. It is rutting season—time to fight! Bulls battle each other to attract a mate. First, they scrape the velvet off their racks. Velvet carries nutrients to the antlers.

Bulls fight by butting heads. Then they shove hard. Losers run away. After the rut, moose migrate to their winter range. They will fight off wolves. They will survive on hard twigs.

On average, moose live 10 to 12 years. The oldest moose on record reached 22 years old.

Chapter 4

A FUTURE FOR MOOSE

Icy night winds blow across the highway. Traffic roars. Headlights whoosh past several moose. They are migrating. The road blocks their path. One moose tries to cross. Horns blare. Brakes screech! Highways, railroads, fences, cars, dogs, and people. These things are all hazards to moose. As human development grows, moose populations shrink. Three-quarters of North America's moose have died off since the 1990s. Experts estimate only one million moose remain.

The western United States loses one football field of wilderness every 2.5 minutes.

Climate change is also a problem. Temperatures are hotter. Heat makes moose tired. They nap in the shade rather than eat. Skinny moose cannot survive winter. Warmer winters bring less snow. Hungry wolf packs easily kill more moose. Warmer weather favors bugs and parasites. They harm healthy moose. Other pests attack the trees that shade moose. Bark beetles in Wyoming destroyed more than one million acres (405,000 ha) in 2009.

Moose have a hard time breathing when temperatures rise above 57 degrees Fahrenheit (14°C).

People can save moose from going **extinct**. Ranchers can use “friendly” fences. They have no barbed wire. Barbs cut moose. They have gaps for calves to crawl through. Some highways have animal crossings. These tunnels or bridges save many moose. **Conservation** groups share smart outdoor tips. For instance, keep dogs leashed when hiking in moose country. Giant action is needed to save these forest giants.

THUMBS UP FOR MOOSE SAFETY

If you see a moose in the wild, stay back. Moose attack when they feel threatened. What is a good distance? Use the wilderness Rule of Thumb. Stretch out your arm. Then give a thumbs-up. Does your thumb cover the moose and its antlers? Perfect. You are at a safe distance.

BEYOND THE BOOK

After reading the book, it's time to think about what you learned. Try the following exercises to jump-start your ideas.

THINK

FIND OUT MORE. Moose are a big topic. There is so much more to discover about them. What else do you want to learn? Look them up on the web, or check out a book from the library. Visit a national park or wildlife ranger station in areas where moose live to learn more.

CREATE

ART TIME. Can you draw a moose? Look up a picture and grab some markers and paper. Which moose habitat will you draw? What is your moose doing in that area? Maybe it is swimming. The sky is the limit!

SHARE

THE MORE YOU KNOW. Share what you learned about North American moose. Use your own words to write a paragraph. What are the main ideas of this book? What facts from the book can you use to support those ideas? Share your paragraph with a classmate. Do they have any comments or questions?

GROW

HELP OUT! Many animals around the world are struggling to survive. Find an organization that is trying to save your favorite animal. Can you volunteer? Can your family donate to the organization's mission? You can also help by telling people about the animal. The more people who help, the more the animal can be protected.

RESEARCH NINJA

Visit www.ninjaresearcher.com/7270 to learn how to take your research skills and book report writing to the next level!

DIGITAL LITERACY TOOLS

Research

SEARCH LIKE A PRO
Learn how to use search engines to find useful websites.

FACT OR FAKE
Discover how you can tell a trusted website from an untrustworthy resource.

TEXT DETECTIVE
Explore how to zero in on the information you need most.

SHOW YOUR WORK
Research responsibly–learn how to cite sources.

DOWNLOADABLE BOOK REPORT FORMS

Write

GET TO THE POINT
Learn how to express your main ideas.

PLAN OF ATTACK
Learn prewriting exercises and create an outline.

Further Resources

BOOKS

Gregory, Josh. *Moose*. New York: Children's Press, 2016.

Lynch, Wayne. *Wildlife of the Rockies for Kids*. Leaside, Ontario, Canada: Fitzhenry & Whiteside, 2022.

May, Julian. *The Big Island: A Story of Isle Royale*. Minneapolis, MN: University of Minnesota Press, 2021.

WEBSITES

FACTSURFER

Factsurfer.com gives you a safe, fun way to find more information.

1. Go to www.factsurfer.com.
2. Enter "Moose" into the search box and click
3. Select your book cover to see a list of related websites.

Glossary

avalanche: A large mass of snow, ice, or earth that suddenly falls down the side of a mountain

conservation: The protection of forests, wildlife, and natural resources

extinct: No longer found alive

habitats: The places where animals or plants are usually found

migrate: To move to another area or climate at a particular time of year

predators: Animals that hunt and eat other animals

scat: Wild animal poop

yearling: An animal that is one year old, or is in its second year of life

About the Author

Jenny Mason is a story-hunter. She explores foreign countries, canyon mazes, and burial crypts to gather the facts that make the best true tales. She received an MFA in Writing for Children and Young Adults from the Vermont College of Fine Arts. She also holds an MPhil from Trinity College Dublin. You will often find her hiking in the Colorado woods where moose roam.

Index

PHOTO CREDITS

The images in this book are reproduced through the courtesy of: Tom Tietz/Shutterstock Images, cover; Drakuliren/Shutterstock Images, p. 3; Africa Studio/Shutterstock Images, p. 4; Michael Liggett/Shutterstock Images, p. 4–5; Imfoto/Shutterstock Images, p. 7 (top); JacobLoyacano/Shutterstock Images, p. 7 (bottom); Anton-Burakov/Shutterstock Images, p. 8 (circle); Uwe Bergwitz/Shutterstock Images, p. 8; Shutterstock Images, p. 9; B.Jaunberzina/Shutterstock Images, p. 10; Mark Byer/Shutterstock Images, p. 10–11; Green Mountain Exposure/Shutterstock Images, p. 12; Dennis W Donohue/Shutterstock Images, p. 14; David Gonzalez Rebollo/Shutterstock Images, p. 15 (top); acavemancandoit/Shutterstock Images, p. 15 (bottom); Imfoto/Shutterstock Images, p. 16; Jasper Jim/Shutterstock Images, p. 17; Sean Neilson/Shutterstock Images, p. 18; Dennis Stogsdill/Shutterstock Images, p. 19; Eivor Kuchta/Shutterstock Images, p. 20–21; meunierd/Shutterstock Images, p. 22; Ludmila Ruzickova/Shutterstock Images, p. 22–23; Andrew Orlemann/Shutterstock Images, p. 24; CSNafzger/Shutterstock Images, p. 25; Wirestock Creators/Shutterstock Images, p. 26; Petr Salinger/Shutterstock Images, p. 27; Krakenimages.com/Shutterstock Images, p. 27 (hand); David Gonzalez RebolloShutterstock Images, p. 31.